Six-Word Lessons

For Project Managers

100 Six-Word Lessons to Make You a Better Project Manager

Lonnie Pacelli

Leading on the Edge International

6wordlessons.com

Six-Word Lessons For Project Managers – 6wordlessons.com
Marketing by Consetta Creative Publicity – consettapr.com
Editing by Patty Pacelli – pattypacelli.com

Copyright © 2009 by Leading on the Edge™ International
704 228th Avenue NE #703
Sammamish WA 98074
leadingonedge.com

ISBN-10: 1-933750-19-7
ISBN-13: 978-1-933750-19-4

L egend has it that Ernest Hemingway was challenged by some friends to write a story in six words. Hemingway responded to the challenge with the following story: *For sale: baby shoes, never worn.*

The story tickles the imagination. Why were the shoes never worn? Were they too small? Did the baby die? Was the baby not able to wear shoes? Any of these are plausible explanations left up to the reader's imagination.

This style of writing has a number of aliases: postcard fiction, flash fiction, micro fiction, and sudden fiction. A dear friend of mine, Tom Fowler, introduced me to this style of writing over a cup of coffee. I was entranced with the style of writing and started thinking about how this extreme brevity of writing could apply in today's micro-burst communication culture of text messages, tweets, and wall posts. Thus the inspiration for **Six-Word Lessons**.

In **Six-Word Lessons** you'll get a bevy of wisdom nuggets with a practical explanation of how to apply the nuggets in your day-to-day routine. Rather than pore through pages and pages of content trying to mine nuggets, **Six-Word Lessons** gives them to you straight up; no strainer needed.

My hope is that you're able to mine some great take-aways from **Six-Word Lessons** and improve how you do things day-in and day-out. Tell me how it's impacted you at story@6wordlessons.com.

Six-Word Lessons for Project Managers

Table of Contents

Six-Word Lessons for Project Managers

Know the Problem, Define the Need

1

Can't write down problem, kill project.

If the Project Sponsor cannot clearly articulate the problem, don't bother proceeding.

Get the sponsor or designee to physically write down the problem statement for all to understand.

2

Sponsor feels problem pain, project on!

Projects that are worth doing mean the sponsor feels some pain that the project can cure.

Make sure you have the right sponsor who feels the benefit of project success and the pain of status quo.

3

Team doesn't understand problem. Build what?

When the team doesn't understand the problem the likelihood of a satisfactory solution is left to chance.

Take the time to ensure the team understands the problem the way the sponsor understands the problem.

4

Sponsor doesn't care about problem. Thud.

A problem that is no longer on the sponsor's radar means it will die a slow death.

Things change. Make sure the sponsor still considers the problem a priority and one which needs to be fixed now.

5

Requirements unclear: team gets to decide.

Unclear requirements leave too much interpretation up to the team which results in building the wrong solution.

Take the time to ensure the requirements are clearly understood and agreed upon among all parties.

6

Bad requirements: do bad stuff faster.

Poorly written requirements can cause you to build a solution that just does stupid things faster.

Don't accept requirements which are of poor quality or don't focus on solving the stated problem.

7

Requirements are outdated. Still using microfilm?

Requirements written eons ago may not apply in the world here and now and very likely won't meet the current need.

Do take advantage of work previously done; just make sure the requirements are relevant for today and tomorrow.

8

Business evolves. Do requirements keep up?

Business changes cause even the most current requirements to change; ignoring change means weak solution.

Be cognizant of sudden or anticipated changes and ensure the requirements reflect the new business environment.

9

Problem not measurable. Solution not doable.

A problem that cannot be quantified makes solving the problem highly subjective and more subject to failure.

Ensure there are clear and objective criteria for knowing that the problem was solved. No squishy criteria.

Design the Solution, Meet the Need

10

Solutions include strategy, people, process, technology.

Too often solutions center on technologies. Technologies are the enabler, not the hub of the solution.

Know your business strategy, your desired to-be process and people goals, and then leverage technology.

11

Think "good enough." Don't gold plate.

It is so easy for project teams to get caught up in "cool factor" and increase scope beyond the business need.

Resist the temptation to synthesize requirements which over-reach the need. Think "good enough."

12

Custom versus packaged. We are "different."

Technologists frequently take a stance of developing customized solutions versus configuring packaged solutions.

Be open-minded when evaluating packaged solutions; let the requirements drive good enough decisions.

13

Beta technologies: first off the cliff.

It's cool to be bleeding edge with new technologies. Not having stood the test of time could be problematic.

Sometimes it makes sense to use beta technologies; do articulate the risks in doing so and decide based on the facts.

14

Wrong technology: the slipper doesn't fit!

At times chosen technologies are a poor fit due to misunderstood, absent or ignored requirements.

No technology is going to meet 100% of the requirements. Know the gaps and decide how best to handle them.

15

Prototypes envision how things could be.

It's difficult for stakeholders to see how a solution will meet needs from requirements and flowcharts.

Make good use of systems prototypes to communicate the to-be people, process and technology systems.

16

Misinterpreted requirements: I didn't expect t*hat*!

The best written requirements could get lost in translation when it comes to developing a solution.

Keep the communication open with stakeholders and avoid assuming too much when interpreting requirements.

17

Manual procedures: we'll design them later.

Too often technologies are developed and thrown "over the wall" for stakeholders to work out procedures.

Ensure there is a clear understanding of how people will do their jobs using technologies <u>and</u> manual procedures.

18

Job changes:
I've gotta do w*hat?*

Procedural and systems changes could very well mean changes in job roles and responsibilities.

Articulate how people's jobs will be impacted and ensure job descriptions are revised accordingly.

Manage to Scope, Avoid the Creep

19

Know functional, geographical, and organizational scope.

Project scope often gets micro-focused on the functional guidelines and less so on geography and organizations.

Paint clear project base-paths and outline the functional, geographic and organizational scope of the project.

20

Good PMs don't boil the ocean.

Over-zealous PMs hyper-focused on pleasing their sponsor at times are too eager to inflate scope.

Keep scope right-sized to the problem statement and use seasoned advisors to help you not say "yes" too much.

21

Controlling scope isn't just saying "no."

PMs frequently equate controlling scope with saying "no" with no due-diligence on the validity of the request.

It's not just about saying "no" to requests. Understand the request, and the consequence of not doing it first.

22

Sponsor's scope, PM's scope, who wins?

It's easy during the heat of battle for a sponsor and PM to develop independent versions of scope.

Keep clear communication lines open on potential scope changes or misunderstandings and nail them *fast*.

23

Project scope statement changes: who decides?

Scope changes haphazardly defined and accepted spell doom for keeping projects focused on the problem.

Change control boards comprised of the sponsor, stakeholders and project team help keep scope right-sized.

24

Scope addition: more money, more time.

Scope additions without budget or schedule impact mean less contingency or overworked teams.

Know how scope additions will be funded and how they impact project schedule before saying yes.

25

Problem and scope: hand in glove.

As a project progresses it is easy for the team to lose focus on the problem statement and start doing too much.

Keep the problem statement in front of the team and sponsor and ensure the scope aligns to solving the problem.

26

Things change, does scope still fit?

Internal and external business environment changes could drive changes in scope--for good reason.

Be aware of business environment changes and proactively address possible scope issues with the sponsor.

27

Scope exclusions need to be explicit.

Most scope definitions focus on what is *in* scope leaving "gray area" for items that could be perceived as in or out.

Seek out the gray areas with the sponsor and stakeholders and specifically decide if they are in or out of scope.

Budget and Schedule, the PM's Compass

28

Project management software saves your butt.

Thinking you can effectively manage a complex project using the likes of Excel or Word is just plain stupid.

Decide upon and implement an appropriate PM software package and learn how it can effectively help you.

29

Critically manage the project critical path.

Not knowing the critical path through a project means not knowing whether you're ahead, behind, or doomed.

Clearly understand task dependencies and those that can slip or not slip without impacting the completion date.

30

Schedule constraints: the doable becomes undoable.

A well-defined scope can't save a project that has misaligned expectations of delivery.

Articulate the scope/schedule misalignment and identify alternatives to reduce scope or elongate schedule.

31

One task, one person, one week.

A task assigned to "the team" or with a duration of more than one week has a greater likelihood of not finishing on time.

Define tasks with a singular owner accountable for delivery and with a schedule duration of one week or less.

32

Resource loading avoids the 500-hour week.

A project schedule which hasn't been resource loaded means some team members will work 500-hour weeks.

Assign singular owners to each task, review assignments, and adjust assignments to evenly distribute work.

33

Didn't include that in budget. Yikes!

It's easy for a PM to think best case when constructing a budget...then get burned when it doesn't happen.

Be realistic about estimating the budget but don't pad the numbers to a point where credibility is questioned.

34

Estimate to complete isn't remaining budget.

Inexperienced PMs tend to subtract actual budget spent from total budget to derive ETC which likely isn't true.

Make sure estimate to complete is an aggregate of remaining work on project not just what is left in the budget.

35

Project without contingency. You kidding me?

At times, to bring a plan on schedule or at budget, a PM will reduce budget or schedule contingency to "make it fit."

Projects are no place for "Hail Mary" acts. Include an agreed-upon budget and schedule contingency.

36

No contingency left. Where'd it go?

PMs rarely track consumption of budget and schedule contingency. It's either there or gone.

In each status report show how much of a project's budget and schedule contingency has been consumed.

Risks and Issues Obliterate Best Plans

37

Risks and issues, what's the difference?

Risks and issues commonly get lumped together and managed only when the poop is about to hit the fan.

Risks need to be mitigated to avoid their becoming issues. Issues are problems which need to be dealt with.

38

Risk management, not cover your butt!

Risks grow out of project assumptions. Many PMs use assumptions as an, "I told you so" if the project goes south.

Risks need to be actively managed in regular status reporting and assessed as to whether the risk is coming true.

39

Great risk mitigation, what, who, when.

Simply identifying that a risk exists is not doing nearly enough to ensure the risk doesn't impact the project.

Good risk mitigation articulates what the mitigation is, who owns doing it, and when the risk is no longer a risk.

40

Risk impact: all aren't created equal.

Projects will have many risks; some which can blow it from the water and others that can have little impact.

Articulate and manage the big risks. Don't let the little risks which are unlikely to derail you chew up cycles.

41

Risk mitigated, mission accomplished, or not.

Just because a risk has been mitigated doesn't mean it's completely dead. It could come back with angry eyes.

Be completely sure a mitigated risk has no chance of re-incarnating itself and derailing your project.

42

Don't take issue with project issues.

Good project issues are those which couldn't be avoided. Bad ones happen due to inattentiveness or denial.

Embrace that issues are going to crop up. Track them on your status report and keep them there until resolved.

43

Issue owner: make it go away.

Issues assigned to "the team" with a date of "TBD" and no clear desired resolution result in a project killer.

Issues need to be assigned a specific owner, articulate what resolution looks like, and have a specific date due.

44

Escalated issue: who ya gonna call?

Many PM either don't escalate issues until too late or escalate issues they can resolve on their own.

Actively review an issue and determine if it is above your pay grade to resolve. Then enlist the right person to help.

45

PM cries wolf. PM gets ignored.

PMs who panic over project issues they could (and should) have resolved themselves ultimately get ignored.

It is the PM's job to stay steady at the controls and not panic the team, the sponsor, and the stakeholders.

Sponsors and Stakeholders, Friend or Foe?

46

Only one sponsor, spare the confusion.

A Project with multiple sponsors is like multiple traffic cops in an intersection. Drivers don't know who to listen to.

Projects need one sponsor with final decision-making authority, even if there are multiple groups involved.

47

Difficult decisions: it's no beauty contest.

Sponsors who are afraid or reluctant to make difficult decisions make life particularly tough for the PM.

Projects will expose tough decisions. Sponsors need to make decisions on time and keep the project moving forward.

48

Distant sponsor: he's not here *again*?

Sponsors who chronically miss updates and status briefings are telling the team "you're not important to me."

Sponsors need to enforce a regular status rhythm with the team; then personally be at every meeting.

49

Sponsors have to be wall breakers.

PMs will encounter resistance from other groups or execs who don't want to play ball with the project.

Sponsors need to be prepared to align peers and other execs to project goals and help the PM get her job done.

50

Sponsors as advocates. Ra Ra Ree.

It's not enough for sponsors to display passive approval and support for a project. Apathy is code for disinterest.

Sponsors must champion the project with affected stakeholder organizations to drive cooperation.

51

Stealth stakeholders: where'd *he* come from?

A stakeholder who rears his ugly head halfway in the project has the potential to derail the project.

Take the time to actively identify each stakeholder group and include each in project activities and briefings.

52

Stakeholder roles: you don't decide that!

Stakeholders whose expectations are misaligned with the project team can upset the decision-making apple cart.

Ensure each stakeholder understands her role in the project and where she gets a vote...and where she doesn't.

53

Status briefings too detailed. Time wasted.

PMs typically don't provide the right level of detail at the right frequency to sponsors and stakeholders.

Understand the frequency and level of detail to provide to sponsors and stakeholders; then follow through.

54

Driving accountability: why aren't you done?

PMs will perform to the sponsor's expectations; low expectations will generally be met with low performance.

Sponsors need to have reasonably high expectations of the team and enforce accountability to meeting the bar.

Testing, Testing, Testing: One, Two, Three

55

Testing strategy: the sooner the better.

Many times testing isn't thought about until a project team is in the solution development phase. Too late.

PMs need to drive development of a test strategy while in the requirements-gathering phase to understand scope.

56

Test the requirements to reduce defects.

Requirements that aren't reviewed for testability leave too much open for interpretation and error.

All requirements need to be reviewed for testability. If you don't know how to test it you can't develop it.

57

Stakeholder testing: the early warning signal.

Frequently stakeholders aren't allowed to user test the solution until after systems testing. Too late.

Assign several stakeholders to do early testing during development to help sniff out problems sooner.

58

Exit criteria: high but reasonable expectations.

Professional testers strive for perfection in establishing exit criteria. Good goal but not always practical.

PMs need to be prepared to drive tradeoffs between exit criteria and schedule pressures among the team.

59

Developers aren't testers. What a load!

Many developers do sub-standard unit testing due to time pressures or just plain laziness.

Establish high expectations with developers to do adequate unit testing; then measure bugs they let through.

60

String testing: diamond in the rough.

String (or integration) testing prior to systems testing tends to get minimized during the development phase.

Structure the work during the development phase so that logical chunks can be string tested early.

61

Bug triage: it's working as designed!

A poorly defined test bug review process results in a buggy system as well as frustrated stakeholders.

Define a timely triage process, ensure all bugs get reviewed, and each bug resolution is agreed upon by the team.

62

Manual procedures must be tested too.

Technologists tend to focus more on testing the technology. If procedures don't work, the user can't do his job.

System Testing needs to encompass how the user wants to use the system, which includes manual procedures.

63

Don't cook the bug count books.

Valid system bugs can be inappropriately deferred or closed to meet acceptance criteria goals.

A bug is a bug regardless of how it is classified. If you run out of time then either relax criteria or slip schedule.

Training: Why Don't You Get It?

64

Training strategy: big effort, little focus.

Core development activities can tend to monopolize a PM's focus, causing her to defer thinking about training.

Outline the training strategy during the requirements-gathering phase to understand its depth and scope.

65

Training includes people, process and technology.

Much of training's typical focus is on how a stakeholder should be using the technology; only one puzzle piece.

Training needs to encompass how a stakeholder will do his job using new processes, technologies and job roles.

66

Sponsors should kick off training sessions.

Training sessions which don't generate buzz and excitement can set a negative wave of sentiment among stakeholders.

Sponsors need to generate buzz in the training session by showing support and excitement about the solution.

67

Developers aren't necessarily the best trainers.

A general view is that those who created the solution can effectively train stakeholders. Bzzzt, wrong.

A developer's skill sets don't always align to those of a trainer. Don't expect developers to be good trainers.

68

Great trainers are great at PR.

Any experienced PM will tell you that an ineffective or incompetent trainer directly influences stakeholder buy-in.

PMs need to ensure trainers effectively represent the solution and create a positive and exciting stakeholder buzz.

69

Right size training to stakeholder needs.

Stakeholders can tend to be either over-trained on unaffected functions or under-trained on relevant functions.

Consciously right-size training on the new solution to what individual stakeholder groups need to know.

70

Do test runs of training sessions.

The most unexpected things tend to happen during training and demos, many of which could be avoided.

Take the time to test and rehearse training sessions with a friendly audience to help work out the kinks.

71

Stakeholders as trainers: big credibility boost.

Trainers who can't relate to the plight of the stakeholder are at risk of minimizing the training experience.

Assign knowledgeable and respected stakeholders who are great communicators to do the training.

72

Design training that's in the moment.

Classroom training is a great way to educate stakeholders, but much can be forgotten after the session is done.

Supplement classroom training with concise and specific online training to help reinforce learning during use.

Vendors and Consultants, Open the Vault

73

Who is that consultant, your friend?

Even a good consultant can be a bad fit for a project. But bad consultants are bad fits for *all* projects.

PMs need to objectively assess their need for a consultant and are better off not using one than using a bad fit.

74

Beware of the bait and switch.

At times vendors and consultants will include strong resumes in proposals who don't actually work on the project.

Get a clear explanation of whether those with strong resumes will be on the project and in what capacity.

75

Billing rates: *how much* are you?

Vendors and consultants naturally feel as if they provide value for the billing, even if others think it's astronomical.

Clearly define what experience level is needed, how much others charge, and how your vendor/consultant aligns.

76

Are you expecting pigs to fly?

Delivery expectations can be sky high because of poor or mismanaged expectation setting.

Establish clear, agreed-upon, and practical expectations with the vendor/ consultant and hold them accountable.

77

Don't let the knowledge walk away.

Vendors and consultants can learn a ton about the solution only to have it dissipate when the vendor leaves.

Put a knowledge transfer plan in place to ensure that what the vendor/ consultant learns doesn't go away.

78

Nonperformers: don't waste my time, dude.

Just because someone works for a vendor or consultant doesn't mean they're going to be a shining star.

PMs need to address vendor/consultant nonperformers quickly before they kill the project.

79

Dueling vendors don't focus on you.

Projects with competing vendors/ consultants risk having them focus on stealing work from each other.

Avoid competing vendors/consultants; if you can't set clear rules for conduct and be willing to fire one if necessary.

80

Make vendors part of the team.

Vendors and consultants who are isolated and treated second-class will not provide the value you expect.

Embrace vendors and consultants as part of the team, let them celebrate success, and feel the weight of issues.

81

Listen to the advice, then decide.

Vendors and consultants can be pretty smart, but shouldn't be blindly followed or ignored.

PMs need to absorb advice and make their own decisions, even if it means firing the vendor/consultant.

Teams that Gel Deliver Once Again

82

Biased PMs: can I trust you?

A PM who shows favor toward a particular person or group risks alienating the rest of the team.

PMs *must* demonstrate objectivity in their team interactions, particularly in multi-organizational teams.

83

Great teams stand unified in public.

Team members that publicly bad-mouth decisions undermine the credibility of the entire team.

PMs need to ensure an environment of healthy debate while reinforcing the need to support decisions publicly.

84

Poor performers must feel the heat.

Team members who don't meet commitments risk destroying the morale and performance of others.

PMs have to publicly and professionally hold team members accountable for delivery.

85

"Not my job" isn't an excuse.

Allowing a project to fail because a team member felt something "wasn't his job" is a pitiful excuse for failure.

PMs should reinforce a "Let's pitch in" ethic to get something done; just avoid repeatedly bailing out a nonperformer.

86

Political animals blow with the wind.

Some team members tend to focus more on politics and personal advancement than project success.

Know who is playing politics. Work to keep them focused on delivery but remove them if they won't cooperate.

87

Empowered leaders can't forget to lead.

Team leaders can either be autocratic in decision making, or in the spirit of empowerment, not drive decisions.

PMs should empower the team to make decisions and own their work, but make tie-breaker decisions when needed.

88

Team meets regularly. Project forges ahead.

Teams that don't meet regularly to discuss project issues, risks and status tend to play tug of war.

Have regular status meetings where the team discusses the project, its problems, and how to push forward.

89

Laughter is the best project medicine.

Teams that bear the weight of the world on their shoulders and don't enjoy a joke are more likely to fail.

PMs need to promote an environment of work balanced with a bit of fun to keep the team motivated and excited.

90

Share the praise, bear the brunt.

PMs who hoard praise, then throw team members under the failure bus don't earn the respect of the team.

PMs must openly share the praise when something good happens and accept accountability for bad stuff.

Adoption: Why Don't They Use It?

91

Communication plans: we're going live *when?*

Internally-facing projects tend to focus more on building the solution and less on communicating to the masses.

Define a clear communication plan of what needs to be communicated, how so, by when, to whom, and why.

92

Solution design reviews: early stakeholder buy-in.

Waiting until the very end to let stakeholders envision the solution means less likelihood of buy-in.

Share the thinking about the solution while in design so stakeholders can influence the solution and feel heard.

.

93

Ignore job impact, create nervous nellies.

Projects that don't specifically communicate job impacts of solutions foster fear, uncertainty and doubt.

Strategically define content and timing of job impacts, particularly where job reductions or changes are involved.

.

94

No executive support means no adoption.

Simply put, projects that don't have full executive support for all affected areas are going to fail.

PMs must know key execs who need to support the solution and use the sponsor to secure support.

95

Solution demonstrations show that it's real.

Stakeholders want to see the solution as early as possible. Hiding it creates skepticism about its readiness.

Do controlled solution demonstrations as soon as the solution is stable enough to show to stakeholders.

96

Town-hall meetings: they ask, you answer.

Projects which avoid ample opportunity for stakeholders to ask questions exacerbate negativity.

Use town-hall meetings as a vehicle to answer questions. Enlist the sponsor to put an exec face on the meeting.

97

Launch countdowns. Three, two, one, blastoff!

As the go-live date approaches, project teams that don't communicate create uncertainty about readiness.

PMs need to create short, frequent communication bursts as launch date approaches to reassure stakeholders.

98

Touch and feels, warm and fuzzy.

Stakeholders want to "play" with the solution as soon as they can. Not being able to do so fosters frustration.

Do touch-and-feels as soon as the solution is stable to let stakeholders experience the solution first hand.

99

Post-launch support: you still there?

Adoption doesn't stop at solution launch. Stakeholders need continued support to keep the launch moving.

Plan for post-launch town-halls, feedback mechanisms, and group chats to secure stakeholder support.

And Number
100...

100

PMs inspire, motivate, and deliver results.

Being a PM isn't just about doing the administration and understanding the mechanics. It's about painting a clear picture of success, enabling team members to perform, removing road blocks, and driving the team to success in a focused and deliberate manner.

See the entire Six-Word
Lesson Series at
6wordlessons.com

Want more great project
management resources?
Check out
projectmanagementadvisor.com

Read more about the author
at **lonniepacelli.com**

3219734

Made in the USA